Upended

ISBN: **978-1-6523643-2-0**

Upended

Poems by

Kathleen Cochran

Wading River Books   Ossining, New York

Wading River Books, Ossining, New York 10562
© 2020 by Kathleen Cochran. All rights reserved.
Printed in the United States of America

Book Designer: Joshua Chapin

Typeface: Cambria Math.

Cover photograph is of Kathleen Cochran with her
father and younger sister, reproduced courtesy of
Kathleen Cochran.

The photograph of Kathleen Cochran is reproduced
courtesy of Kathleen Cochran and Peter Cochran.

Companion previously appeared in *Subtropic 8* (May 2009).

ISBN: **978-1-6523643-2-0.** FIRST PRINTING.

Queries to wadingriverpub@gmail.com

ACKNOWLEDGEMENTS

Many thanks to Estha Weiner, poet and teacher, for her support and encouragement. Thanks also to members of Estha's poetry group, including Lisa Fleck, Phyllis Gutman, Ruth Handel, Judy Ryan, and Mary Jane Motl.

Sandy Chapin and Josh Chapin were instrumental in guiding this collection through design and publication. Maeve Kinkead offered insightful comments and suggestions.

I am grateful to my sons Ben and Sam, who cheered me on. Most especially, I appreciate the contributions of my husband Peter, who generously devoted many hours to helping me complete this project.

CONTENTS

For Peter

Vienna, 1936

Christmas Eve when she is 17,
the Christkindl leaves her
Gone with the Wind.

Enthralled, she sprawls
on the divan,
devours the book,

never guessing this story
is a window onto Christmas
yet to come. Candles burn

on the tree.
Snow falls on Stefansdom.
Strauss waltzes swell

at the Opera Ball.
Her beaux
sip champagne

from her slipper,
squire her home,
leave her to dream

of the next ball
and the next,
while they sally forth

to meet
their streetwalkers,
their shopgirls.

We Leave Post-War Europe

Photo on shipboard:
father and baby
framed by a porthole.
In profile, he smiles.

I squint at the camera,
look straight through
my mother, through
the lens on her face
out the back of her head,
and across the Atlantic
to twelve years away

where she waits:
iceberg to his Titanic.

Pineapple, Munich, 1949

Promise of sweetness,
chilled disk on a
round white plate,

empty cutout where the core
was reamed out clean
in a silver chrome factory

somewhere in the U.S., army-sized
tins shipped to military bases
overseas, a taste of home.

Now a mound of whipped cream
slides off the spoon held by the
smooth hand of a sister of Mercy,

head bowed as in prayer. Gravely,
she tastes, surrenders to the contrast
of sweet-tangy fruit and rich cream;

closes her eyes. *Delicious.*
The baby's mother smiles.
Her gift to you. The baby yearns

toward the mother's voice,
pink baby skin, blue
incoherent newborn eyes,

small universe unto herself
in this white ward filled with
black-and-white nuns,

yellow pineapple
and ivory cream from the
commissary at the base,

where the baby's father
parlayed prestige into dessert
for the sisters who gave

safe passage to his infant
daughter in this hospital
surrounded by twisted

buildings, cratered roads
motherless children,
borders sharp as shrapnel.

Rotary

Long before WiFi, dearest,
index fingers
wore a path around the dial—slow-dragged
clockwise, then released: click-click-click,
2 so quick.
9 took its time, rode the tension back around,
clattered like Venetian blinds.

Even though I tucked myself behind the door
next to the telephone table (it had its own table)

my mother knew who I was calling
by the sound of the whirs.

Pink

News of my old high school's closing
takes me back to pink:
the shocking pink linen shift

my mother sewed for me.
I chose the color—the juicy
watermelon-pink cardigan

that was my "I'm OK" armor
in the high school world of
sweetheart rose fashion princesses

decked out in Villager dresses
and matching Capezio shoes,
pastel rainbow feet in the hallways.

I had one pair, in a shade
composed of canteloupe and tangerine,
the pink of orange, soft as butter,

with flat heels and no support,
and I didn't care that my feet
were hot and red and sweaty,

by the time I walked the
Florida mile and a half home, while
ivory girls with bouffant flips

and cheerleader smiles and gold circle pins
rolled past me in the open-windowed city bus,
on their breezy way home to candy pink rooms

with white princess phones;
bulging closets, fluttery mothers,
strawberry milk shake lives.

Florida, 1956

i

They arrive in the morning,
leave before supper. Yard
men, faces hidden by hat brims,
rake and weed, clip and mow.
Maids bustle in and out.
Wash, iron. Cook, clean.
Their eyes hover like watchful
fish in dark ponds.

Most of their names I do not
know. The ones at my house are
Arthur and Magnolia. Outside,
Arthur talks to me.

Inside, Magnolia talks at no one
in particular.

ii

Magnolia takes our grown-up
Easter chicks. They complain
in a box in our car. "Where will
you keep them?" I ask.

My mother's fake coughing fit
cuts off Magnolia's reply, tells me
these chickens will not be un-
happy for long.

My mother believes I'd be sad if
she told me our chickens will fry.
She thinks her distraction worked.
Wrong on both counts.

She thinks she knows what I think.
I let her think that.

Home Birth

My mother's voice, urgent:
Bill, she is coming.
Father, outbackdoor,
to me: *Do not move.*

Pink grapefruit glistening,
halfway to mouth, my
four-year-old arm suspended in air.
Don't move, don't;
Don't move.

Inbackdoor stumbling,
dumbstruck neighbor ladies
mime fear, agitation;
wild red-rimmed eyes
roll in pale morning masks;
bathrobes, curlers, slippers;
kabuki housewives,
ghostly procession
blows past in a gust.

Moans and commotion,
My mother's voice implores and commands:

Hold her up, hold her
up, let me
see, hold her up.
Hold—her—up.

Sounds subside;
neighbor lady, restored,
once more human, smiles,
holding small bundle
wrapped up in a towel.
Tiny head,
just the top,
pearly pink.

Baby.
Sister.
My baby
sister. My
sister, for
me. Mine,
baby sister.
For me.

Neighbor

An insect, my neighbor, perched prayerful
on our back door step, head just inches

from the bathroom window. I press
against the cool tile wall, stiller than still,

willing myself so quiet, so flat, he will not know
I'm here. But the high whine of his wings says

he knows. Brittle legs rub together; bulging
mantis eyes slide in my direction, greedy

slantways look, while his pretend human voice
says, *Hello neighbor, coming to church?*

A deacon at the Baptist church: staid, pious,
reverent. Neighborhood girls know better.

Impish sisters, two doors down, rollicking
Salomes, dance naked in their window

to torment him. Mantis rustles in
shrubbery at twilight, cannot look away.

The men don't like him but don't know why.
The women think him harmless. One day

my sister and her friend, mothers in the kitchen,
let slip the truth about the sneaky green creature

next door. In unison, the women say
His wife must never know.

I see him listening as they speak, in some
hidden place: hungry, waiting, as images of

budding breasts, little-girl clefts sear
his sensors and he whirs, he sings.

At work his wife, kneeling, fits Sunday
shoes to Baptist feet, dreams of a new

Frigidaire. The mothers pour coffee and
exchange glances. The fathers carry

their suspicions in their briefcases.
And we neighborhood girls

keep watch while we play, stay
clear of this creepy, thrumming bug

as one by one, we grow up and go,
leave him to his reverie, alone.

Dallas: November 22, 1963

I heard the news
from Reba Bray.
I was going up
the stairs, she
was coming down.
Her face bobbed like a beach ball
on a sea of blue-jean legs,
rode waves of frothy petticoats.
Her words ricocheted
in the stairwell.
Nobody believed her.

*Everything keeps going and everything stops. The momentum
of the thing that's happened picks up, though the engine's cut off.*

We went to class,
learned it was true.
The President was shot.
Then he was dead.
Early dismissal.
I walked
empty sidewalks,
carless streets.
The sun glared,
the air hung oddly,
shimmered and swelled.
Otherworldly confetti
glittered, suspended,
over a parade, a float,
a marching band
that wasn't there.
In my head,
a ghost trombone.

*Earth's axis totters. Watch TV until you're dizzy, spin until you drop. Float up,
look down from your orbit. Images burrow inside, rewire your brain.*

The book depository,
looking like a high school.
The assassin, looking
like he'd hang out
with the smokers
and the easy girls.
His mouth would taste
of tobacco and menthol.
See the moment
of his death, the moment of
the murderer's murder.
See the pink pillbox hat
in the motorcade, floating
on a river of cars.
like stylish kitchens
of the day, pink and gray,
blood and brains.

Three Moons

Poet Moon

An acclaimed poet
has come to my aunt's college.
I go to hear him read before he dies.
His famously abundant thatch of silver hair
floats like the moon in the pines. 85 years
he has been gathering moonlight,
collecting species and subspecies:
Aloof, faraway,
frost-flecked pumpkin moon.
Twirling, thumping beer hall polka moon.
Playful moon-child swinging
from branch to black branch,
running up and down
ladders of light.

Party Moons

After the reading,
my aunt throws a party.
Candles and lanterns
dot the house and garden.
Students sing and play guitar.
Where have all the flowers gone?
Blowing in the wind.
Couples drift into dark corners.
Their glowing cigarettes,
little personal moons,
go with them.
People fuss over me,
slip me sips of beer.
P.S. I'm the only ninth grader here.

Albino Moon
My aunt puts me on the bus home.
Sit in the front, she says. *Promise.*
I promise, then go all the way to the back.
In Starke, two boys get on, one skinny and
sharp-faced; one soft and dead white with pink eyes.
He takes the seat in front of mine, turns to look,
slack-jawed moon face hovering over the seat back.
My mother would have called him a half-wit.
My mother would have smacked Skinny
for feeling my leg while Half-Wit waited for
what never happened, because I got Skinny talking
and what he wanted more than his fingers up my thigh
was to tell me all about himself in the back of the bus
as the fierce Florida sunset faded into a moonless night.

Jade East

I was 16, stashed
in a dorm while my mother
took off for graduate school
and my dad learned
to live alone.

He was from Jersey, a guy other guys
called by his last name. Shouts of "Hey!
Waclawski!"—rhymed with
house key—announced he was near.
I already knew from the air.

Citrus, cedarwoods,
florals, musk, vanilla.
Recommended use: evening.
Not to mention morning, noon, and night.
I could have smelled him clear across
the river under the neon cup atop
the Maxwell House packing plant
on the edge of downtown,
near my dad's office.

I loved his smile, his height, his blue
blue eyes that knew I was smitten, knew
he could get what he wanted.
We sat, heads close, in a vacant lecture hall.
I rescued dangling modifiers, got his subjects
and verbs to agree. He bestowed
a brief, chaste kiss, then

moseyed off to shoot pool
with some Phi Delts.
I gathered my books,
crossed the twilight campus,
savored the fading fragrance
of his leaving.

her bad

she's going out
saturday night
tattoo, tongue ring,
torn black tights
running through
those headlight
stripes
who's she smiling
for tonight

some bad boy

he's a poet
plays the bass
skinny body
skinny face
looks at her like
he can erase
that goth girl outfit,
looks like he knows how
she looks without it

that bad boy,
bad bad bad.

sits in health class
texting him
dreams it's Saturday again

lives to get her hands
on him, taste his cigarettes
and gin, smoke his
weed and listen in
while he trash talks
with his friends
thinks one day she'll
marry him

that bad boy
she loves that bad
boy wants that
bad boy wants
him bad.

hasn't figured
out the problem:
if she gets him
she won't want him
real bad boys
can't be had
once you got'em
they're not bad.

Top Forty

Transistor radio, tan leather case,
loop to hang it from a handlebar,
sings to me while I bike the streets
of Jacksonville, near and far.

I get around. I met him at the candy store.
Woke up this morning feeling fine.
And the sun's gonna shine in my back door some day.

Back door to my kitchen, left behind
while I cruise, hair flying,
on my Western Auto Liberation
two wheeler, and I am free.
Let the women come and go.
Let them talk about what they like.
Let them talk about me.
Get the picture? Yes, we see.

If you're lonely, then it's your blues.
Don't ask me to take care of you.
Because the sun's gonna shine in my back door some day.

Unsuitable boys with cigarettes and
slicked-back hair.
Tobacco taste on someone else's tongue.
My social life is causing
some despair. I am having fun, fun, fun,
twisting the night away.

I don't care what the people say.
The sun's gonna shine in my back door some day.

Back Story

Who are you? Incongruous
embodiment of imaginings
past, fabled admirer, swain,

lover. You were the reason
I had to dish up some
lies along with supper

that night, and it was late,
and the foolproof never-fail
meat sauce burned, because I did not
pay attention,
no, the chef, age 12 did
not attend,
wondering when her
mother would appear.

So dinner had
not yet begun
when she swooped

through the back door,
nostrils flaring,
sucking in the
aroma of blackened
tomato sauce hard-glued
to heavy aluminum pan,

no nostick then,
and she stuck to me
yes she stuck.

And it was my
fault, yes mine,
my fault

that the dinner was ruined and she,
she had to do it all, Do It
All Herself.

Meanwhile, where were you?
Who waited up, who fed
you, and what?

Your children—were they
Home? I knew
their names.

And the alcoholic wife, was she
awake? Or passed out
cold, rehearsing her demise?
And I wish I didn't
know you now;
wish I could erase you.
And I fear your
past as I fear

your death,
and I miss you
before you are gone.

And I wish
I didn't like you
so much.

Air Hunger

Midnight train:
The engine has your face.

Light streams
from wide blank eyes.
Toothless mouth
bites at air you crave
but can't inhale.

Nights long ago,
train whistles mixed
with your laughter
while you played cards
with the neighbors.

Next day there would be
leftover cake, lipstick
on cup rims, predictable
as trains. Now you roam
the tracks, seeking oxygen.

I watch you go.

Homage to Bob

*It doesn't matter
where you leave things
they aren't there when
you come back.*
    *-Robert Breer
        experimental
        filmmaker, painter,
        and sculptor*

You leave your credit card
on the table at the café
by the metro in the seizieme.
This being France—
land of stealthy incremental animation—
when you return
the table has gone over to the rival café across the street;
the credit card slid into a flower pot;
the fat unfettered sausage flees the egg-flecked plate,
skedaddles down the boulevard
while somewhere a flaneur
about to bite into his crocque-monsieur
explodes, leaves a grease spot on the wall
next to the autographed photo
of Yves Montand.

Angel Babcock

Twister took her,
peeled open the trailer
like it was a tin
of sardines. Sucked out its insides,
father, mother, three kids—
swirled them, churned them
in its terrible gullet,

Spat them out into a field.
Angel flew farthest.
Grandfather spotted her,
scrap on the ground. Not yet dead.

Grandmother held her,
sang "Itsy Bitsy Spider,"
turned off the life support.
Gave her up.

Girls

In defiance of Donna, Mama prepared
extra meals to heat up over Sterno.

My sister and I tracked the color of the air,
watched the sky turn dull green,

sat glued to the transistor radio
while the wind rustled, built to a roar,

kept abreast of where the eye was,
not to be taken in by its false peace.

After Dora, my dad drove us all to the beach
to see hunks of seafoam big as cars.

By Camille, the family was blown apart.
My father braved ensuing storms alone.

Hugo would be his last. He died in '90,
never to know about Sandy, never to hear

of storm surge; wasn't there to remind us
the eye of the storm is its peak of danger.

Slideshow: Sandy

Half under water,
cars wallow
and list
in Rockaway.

Boats, upended,
teeter
in Breezy
Point backyards.

Up and down
the Jersey shore
broken bungalows
buckle, rot.

At Seaside Heights
the roller coaster,
undulating,
slinks out to sea.

Donated clothes
spill from paper bags
onto the sidewalk
like flowers.

Flowers spill
over coffins
of small boys swept
from their mothers' arms.

Mud and debris.
Mud and debris.
National Guard
hands out MREs.

Residents dig
in thirty degrees
to salvage belongings
in Babylon.

May 1979

Days on end, it rained.
The window ledge on Prince
dripped water on the sidewalk.
In green suburbs the ground
collapsed. May turned murderous.
Random killings on Succabone

Road, bullets through bone.
They went house to house in the rain,
raided safes, looted jewels, murdered
the ones they found there, princes
and peons, sent them into the ground.
In Soho on the sidewalk

slicker-clad kids kissed their mothers, from the sidewalk
stepped onto the school bus, chilled to the bone
even though it was May. In Chicago a plane left the ground,
lifted off, crashed in the rain.
And in Soho on Prince,
rain whetted someone's taste for murder:

a watcher and waiter
whose thoughts sprang like weeds in the sidewalk
seized a small blond prince
who would never be found, not one bone.
Still the rain
fell on swings in the playground;

slicked the tarmac; soaked the grounds
of blood-soaked houses where the murders
were fresh. Rain
fell on the sidewalk
where the mothers stood, bone-
tired and terrified, after the prince,

the little lost and disembodied prince,
disappeared as if the ground
had swallowed him, even the bones.
The robins sang "Murder."
Flowers piled up on the sidewalk.
May ended. The sun stopped the rain.

They still speak of his murder on Prince Street.
His face haunts the sidewalks and playgrounds.
The rain searches the dust for his bones.

Breadcrumbs

Utoya Island, 2011

Send them to an island,
your precious children,
robust, bursting
with good will, aglow
with certainty.

Do you notice things
are not what they seem?
The house—gingerbread.
The oven—always set
to bake.

The cook is a cop is a killer.
Breadcrumbs dissolve
in the water.
There's no place like home.
There is no place.

Anders   *Utoya Island, 2011*

He looks like us.
So surely
he must
be OK?

Handsome face,
chiseled head.
His father wishes
he were dead.

Breaths of silent
children wreathe
like fog above
a sea of grief.

Morning Edition: Fifteen Years Later

Names are read. The Fed moves in
on little cat feet, coaxed by
rosy growth scenarios,
promise of Fancy Feast.

The Dow is up, along with the sun.
And—good news! We have the
the safest skyscrapers ever.

Thick, double thick, triple thick concrete
at the core makes for a tower
of unassailable integrity, unless a certain

metropolitan Mephistopheles
with Dreamsicle hair looks the other way
when substandard stuff is poured.

The worst would be to forget.
Never, never forget.

So let the names run in the background
while coffee is brewed. Let each of us
Use the word *hero* at least fifteen times.
The dead were diverse,
So let's finish Taps with a
Jazzy inflection.

Parking rules suspended for religious observation.

We have some troubles on transit.

Right now in Central Park it's 62 degrees at 7:45.

Crazy Eddie is no longer with us.

Verloren

July 11, 2011: In an orthodox Jewish community in Brooklyn,
a young boy walking home alone for the first time lost his way...

Shirtless man,
hideous heat.
In his icebox—
a child's feet.

They are there
when he takes out a beer.
The better to eat you with,
my dear.

Wolf in the forest, wolf
on the street, wolf
in the attic
licking his teeth.

Seven blocks:
horror complete. Grieve
for the missteps
of innocent feet.

House Call

She comes, she comes—the mobile vet—
on her way to kill your pet,
and you're beginning to regret
you called her.

Rat-a-tat—she's at your door,
demure yet businesslike—death's whore—
you want to run from what's in store.
You let her in.

"Visa, Master's fine, as cash is.
Now let's talk about the ashes—
best discussed before he passes."
Dies, you think.

Trip-trap, her footstep on your stair—
old orange cat rests, unaware,
cradled in blankets soft as air.
Don't hurt him.

With her syringe she pricks his side.
He lifts his head, eyes open wide—
he sags, turns limp, as breath subsides,
You watch him go.

She wraps him in a towel—the witch—
collects her lethal bag of tricks.
Another death without a hitch.
Get out.

She's gone. He's gone. House, empty now,
absorbs his plaintive last meow.
You hope she hits a tree, the cow.
You'll manage, though you don't know how.
How can Providence allow
such mercy?

Companion

Discontent is a bony dog,
mangy, whiny, needy.
He craves your care.
He's always there.

Underfoot he trips you,
leaking drool, leaking
pee, licking you.
You need him too.

He's shrill and yappy,
prone to snap.
Leash him tight.
Your knuckles are white.

He's your acid cloud
On a sunny day,
your gall made flesh.
How well you mesh.

Put on your pretty floral gown;
smile, dip, fawn.
He's under your skirt,
gnawing a bone.

You are never alone.

Where the Wild Things Are

Animal World is an elephant
tied to a post
by the highway
in Starke, Florida.
No shelter, no shade, just a concrete slab in shrill sun,
doppler throb as cars approach, recede.
Does she imagine, as dusk falls,
pavement cools, roadsounds dim,
that somewhere down
the long yellow line,
a savannah sprouts,
the rising moon spills light
on ponds edged with soft mud, and they are coming to her,
all of them, the babies and the old ones too—
billowy silhouettes against the flat sky,
they come, call to her, touch her face
with their exquisite trunks. Her chain drops off
and she goes with them, no longer
the last elephant on earth.

Unword

Is it per se forbidden?
What if it's a quote, as in

"Huck Finn traveled
 with Unword Jim."

The Unword isn't just American.
The British used it to signify
that mottled pink potato-pale people
were superior to dark ones, who
were put on earth to wash
their floors and serve them tea.

If you want to capture what it is
to be devalued, demeaned,
and denigrated, if you want
to say how very badly
someone is treated,
then the Unword
is one word that could
do the job.

Except we don't say it
In public. Not if we're white.
Not unless we're bold
as Randy Newman,
sharp as Mark Twain,
and we don't care

if people cease to
look each other
in the eye when
the Unword,
is spoken
out loud.

Waltz for Dead Children

We never stop missing the ones who die early.
Carl, struck by a boat in a lake. At his house I ate cake,
took back a book he had borrowed.

Then Robbie: sweet, shy. We rode bikes together.
A week later, car crash. I wondered: Did he know
he was dying?

Debbie, a cheerleader, short frosted hair. Stopped
eating, they said, and she died. I tried to imagine
her thinness.

Years later, Andrew, my son's age. Laid his head
on the Metro North tracks, left his town with
a permanent ghost.

The ones who lose siblings young wear their loss
quiet as a stone. When they disclose it, you feel
you always have known.

One says: He was two years younger than me—
freckled, funny, droll. It should never have
happened. The doctor messed up.

Another says: My oldest brother drowned. I was conceived
to replace him. I used to sneak looks at pictures of him
in his casket.

Some never do tell: My dad, one of nine—
so he said. After his death, on a family tree,
a tenth name, under my father's.

Boy. Died a year old. My dad kept his memory
deep in his pocket, an old coin
he touched every day.

Yes, the ones who die young never leave us.
On yellowing pages of stained genealogies
typed on Corona portables,

they catch our attention. On gravestones,
their fading names chant themselves faintly.
They float in our minds

like snowflakes so light, before
you can see them, they melt. They visit us
in the lovely and the ordinary:

summer frog song,
dance of freckles
across a grandchild's cheek.

Henry at One Year

Baby blocks,
3-inch cubes
embossed
with animals

of barnyard,
tundra, veldt.
Some would
eat up a baby

if they could.
Soft, nontoxic
vinyl, not hard
wood. I stack

them; make
a tower five
blocks high.
He reaches

out, to topple
them, I think;
but
with grave delicacy,

he fingers them,
feather-brushes
surfaces as if
to read by touch

what holds them
upright; how it is
they stay in place,
don't fall down.

Tribute to Mother with Peacock Baby

-from the sculpture of that name by Sigalit Landau

Merrily you go a-maying,
shoulder high your baby rides,
both your heads elsewhere, decaying,

slipped away down some hillside,
in pinestraw eye to eye a-lying
whilst the path you blithely stride.

If you had ears, then you might hear
as your wee child sits unconcerned
the zing of arrows flying near—

Plainly he no pain discerns:
though sharp points prick him from the rear
his little prick remains upturned.

Headless, heedless, full of grace
lithely arcing, foot extended
you could take Aphrodite's place

if only your sweet head were mended—
or Madonna's, though in that case
your lack of robes would be amended.

Celadon, topaz, rose and azure:
Botticelli's Tuscan palette
colors your divine composure.

In the world that you inhabit
every morsel is ambrosia,
though you lack the mouth to eat it.

On your way, lady beguiling,
you and your pincushion child,
unselfconscious, reconciling

all that's lovely, all that's vile.
Somewhere I swear your heads are smiling
at your courage— beauty—style.

Meteor Shower *Hudson River, November 2001*

We wanted magic,
but they're really just debris.
For this we left a warm bed,

bundled up, drove to the riverside,
trudged to the water's edge,
looking for transcendence.

After a few bright streaks,
reflexive oohs and aahhs crooned
all around by invisible mouths.

We secretly know what
we dare not say: that this
is about as exciting as being

in the bottom of a cosmic ashtray,
while some giant smoker's ash,
flicked in our direction, falls,

disintegrates before it touches down,
cleanly burns. No need
for a celestial dustbuster.

And yet, the fact that we are all here
is enough. Voices in the dark, families
with children, come down in the middle

of the night in order that
the 6-year-old may one day
say, "Remember, back around

the turn of the century,
when we got up
in the pitch dark

and watched the meteor shower,
when we were just babies, and
our parents so young, so strong?"

And so that the image of the meteors
may supplant or at least offset
those other images

of fallings from the sky,
the tall columns downriver
like the long cylindrical ash

of two burnt cigarettes
held upright, keeping
their illusion cigarette

shapes until they
collapse, top down,
crushing the air.

We move and shift. We stand,
we sit. We should have
brought beach chairs. We

should have brought
a blanket. My neck hurts.
My feet are numb.

But we stay, long after
the last meteor has
disappeared behind

the cliffs of the Palisades,
and the children have been
taken home to bed.

Because the real wonder is
the perfect night sky,
the clarity and timelessness of it,

Orion's gleaming belt,
the dusty Pleiades,
still there.

My Son Goes to India

Why not India Land?
Surely there is a building
at Epcot for this—

authentic poori, fake beggars.
And you—you live on Sixth Street,
 where one kitchen, they say,

stocks all the restaurants
on the block with tikkas,
fritters, lassis, dal.

Annette Funicello died. I watched her
on the neighbor's TV set
until we got our own.

You ascend
in a jet to Delhi.
M–I–C... Lockerbie.

K–E–Y, irony—
It's Boston where
the danger is today

and you are safe away
in tomorrow, tethered
to earth and me

by a thread
of wishes,
dust, and gravity.

Come home.

Millennial

I glimpse him traipsing up the wooded path—
trademark orange sneakers, navy hat.
White wires like a bridle on his neck. Music

streams unheard by me, beneath ear flaps.
He looks like fourteen, not thirty-four;
boyish, shy, and skittish as a colt.

Is he remembering Manila before the hurricane?
Is he longing for a cheeseburger and fries?
Or thinking of his Gran, in whose attic

he lives while seeking employment,
The summer past, by accident,
she overdid the anticoagulants.

He tends her like a tender plant,
doles out doses with his own hand;
settles her and, while she naps,

rambles through this extrava-
ganza of symbiosis and decay—

Leaves melt into pungent,
loamy ground.

Crusty lichens cling
to fallen boughs.

Spongy fungi bob and wave
on wispy stalks.

Mosses bounce
with possibility.

I breach the outer borders of his sight.
He startles, throws a nod my way,
picks up the pace and disappears.

Only Child

For this the son,
long gone,
returns—drives

down to DC
week after week,
visits doctors,

washes bedding,
pays bills, pores
over documents,

ponders the merits
of places with names
like Sunrise.

His great-grandfather,
sharecropper, signed
his name with X.

He, Harvard Law,
negotiates with men
so powerful

he's not allowed to know
their names. He sits
among the relics

of his childhood, preserved
by the two whose brains—
with his own—

are the last repository
of the life, here,
that was his:

Wild West wallpaper.
Bucking bronco lamp.

Lydia

Last time I saw Lydia
she was going to a gig
in Brooklyn.

I drove her
to catch the 9
in Riverdale,

Van Cortlandt stop,
end of the line,
but she

wouldn't get out, turned sulky,
tried to bully me
into taking her

all the way to someplace
near Pratt, where she'd
spend the night

on somebody's couch,
finger-brush teeth with
strange toothpaste,

leave a towel
in a wad on the floor.
The old Lydia

would have got
away with it.
Her way

of lighting up
made you forgive her.
Now she's dim

and gray, over- or
under-medicated—
hard to say;

like her guitar case,
seen better days
and at last

she's climbing
the long steep stairs
to tomorrow,

when she will deliver music
enrichment to underserved
third graders.

They will sing *The Cat Came Back*
and it won't add up
to a hill

of beans when it comes
time to calculate
Social Security,

test the kindness
of strangers.

Seer

It's Cassandra
at the intersection,
stepping from a white
steam column,
arm outstretched to
hail a cab.

She glints like a
mirror shard,
schrecklichkeit
of jagged hips,
toothpick arms,
pencil thighs,
meager form
defined by black
stretch pants, red
ruffles at throat,
wrists, waist.

White boots—'70s.
Mask, Delphi. Kohl-
rimmed eyes stare.
Blood-red mouth
gapes. Painted-on
eyebrows arch blankly
on her face stretched tight
as plastic wrap.

Predicting the tummy-roll
cellulite jokes
of the ageless gods,
she has struck pre-emptively,
calling in wielders of knives;
yet every scoop and slice,
each tug and tightening
brings her closer to the
bone, foreshadowing
the fate we all await,
from which we avert
our eyes.

Poor prophet, never heeded.
She meets your gaze
for an instant,
then she's gone,

melted into the noise
and the fumes. You
head for the Number 4 train,
underground.

Parts of Speech

Oncologist (noun)
a doc you don't want
in your email.

Metastasize (verb)
slithers soft,
like a fraudulent friend.

Stage (noun):
an unpleasant time
in your teens.

Stage 4 (adjective)
makes you wish
you were thirteen again.

Chemo, chemo
(noun, noun)—the steady
drip drip of slow poison.

Biweekly (adverb):
thug; mugger
who steals half your life.

Undergoing:
Hold on to the tenuous
parachute (gerund).

(Pronoun) You,
falling through
whatever is left.

The Lyrics of The Bonjour Tristesse Brassiere Company

The lyrics of the Bonjour Tristesse Brassiere Company
Won't come to me.
Deep in my formerly accessible
brain they hide, defy retrieval,
make me wild.

You'd think one song fewer
in my treasury of singable delights
would be no big deal.

Well, it's killing me: can't bear
to think it's gone.
When I'm blue,

what'll I do? Belt out *Barbara Ann*?
Intone the nah-nah-nah
of *Hey Jude*?

I ache for what I've lost.
So what if Google's bots
can find the words

whose absence
twists me
like a cruller.

Take me back
where I can be me,
at least momentarily.

Bonjour, tristesse.
C'est la vie.
Whatever.

September Song

twisted limbs, razor moon

withered leaves and cry of loon

ashen air and branches bare
fair is foul and foul is fair
beware, beware
the fall.

Midsummer's Eve

Fireflies,
legions of them,
take command
of the dark.

From the meadow's
shallow bowl
to the tops
of oaks and willows,
they quiver, swoop,
flicker, gleam;
silver the night.

In their world, what are we—
you, me, the dog?
Maybe we figure
as a vague warmth,
an unidentifiable heaviness
at the edge of their lightfest—
observers, incidental
to the show.

Narcissi

i

Hardest winter ever,
relentless cold, never-melting
snow, a gift from
something called
the Polar Vortex,
rhymes with Goretex,
rhymes with more sex,
which is what we should be having
these leaden nights that push the stars away.

Instead, our so-called comforter
presses down like sheetrock.
We sleep like death.

ii

April, my darling, yes: Spring. Temps leap into the 70s.
Daffs ripple on the hill. We go to bed believing
we are safe, the brutal season's slunk back to its cave.
New green tendrils intertwine; we vibrate
to the slip and wrap of them. And then—
the hiss of sleet. You release me, groan,
pull the pillow over your face. Narcissi, desperate,
lie splayed on icy ground, hope to keep their heads.
In the morning, there will be a dusting of snow,

frozen slush in yellow crowns,
King Alfred daffsicles
trying to melt.

Newcomb Hollow Beach

There is always a child
smooth as sea glass,
rapt
in sand's pliancy,
lost
in sand's grit,
entranced
by how sand
gives back
what is given—

imprint of
thigh, shape
of bucket—

child complete
as a clam,
immersed in sea
rhythm—waves
      ripple, roll,
    stride long-fingered notes,
    beach keyboard resonates,

flows without words—

always, a mother
casts her voice
through late
slant sun:
it's time it's time.
Child scrambles up,
all arms and legs,
runs willing
to dinner,
nightfall, the
fathomless future.

Snow

Let it come.
Let it gather damp and opaque,
smoothe away glare with emollient grays.
Let it settle like lint on the overcoat
of the buyer of the last loaf of bread,
who scurries across the deserted parking lot
as first flakes swirl. Let pavement

turn white; houses, trees, white; air, white;
thought, white. Let every sentient being

be delivered from intention,
obligation, routine—watch

snow fall with no idea
save the idea of snow.

New York Ultrasound

Prenatal vertebrae
on velvet black,

fairy lights
     festooning trees
     along Fifth Avenue—

looping strands
     that limn the Verrazano
     on a no-moon night—

like a constellation arcing
     over phosphorescent waters
     off Long Island—

bubbles rising
     through the Hudson's
     briny depths—

small pearl bones unfurl
from where they come from,
stretch towards where they go.

13 Ways Clouds Have of Being Looked At

1. Creamy dessert:
   meringue, zabaglione,
   ile flottante
   in a bowl
   of cerulean

2. Wild stallion:
   barrel-chested steeds
   seethe— manes stream,
   muzzles foam,
   unbridled.

3. Cirrus circus:
   high-jumping, tail-
   wagging toy poodles
   bound through hoops
   with calliope ease.

4. Blanket clubhouse:
   Thick cotton batting,
   puffy, channel-stitched,
   heavy-light descends
   as feathers fly.

5. Skyskin blister:
   Grey-yellow blotches
   dot the perfect prom-blue
   sky, make the rising moon
   despair.

6. Deception meadow:
   On sky-field
   of opalescent jade,
   lambs dance.
   Or are they ducks?

7. Scavenger mouth:
   Ragged, wheeling,
   voracious; sniffs the ground,
   touches down,
   sucks up everything,

8. Water-mirror:
   Where sea ends
   and clouds begin,
   no telling. Even seals
   don't know.

9. Sparkle dead-alive:
   Preserve a dead crow's
   body. Glue glassy crystals
   all over it. Barbaric glass
   crow-cloud.

10. Shadow-rug: unrolled,
    admitting sun beneath,
    makes shadows loom—
    or blocking sun, makes
    shadows disappear.

11. Sunset flame-pool:
    orange-red atop a vast
    and deepening
    black. Fire
    on an oil field.

12. Royal commander:
    towering, sky-filling
    mass of amethyst and ermine,
    at its crown backlit,
    edged violet and gold.

13.   Your verse here.

Approximate Wait Time Will Be

I can't get through; the line is always blocked.
I'm stuck inside a looping message, mute.
I spin wheels, spin tales, mark time, and pretend
That this is not a purposeless pursuit.
While I wait for you, I'm growing old.
We thank you for your patience while on hold.

Mummified, cocooned, I keep my post.
Inaction is my choice and chooses me.
No reason to expect to be released.
If I disconnect, will I be free?
So many stories waiting to be told.
We thank you for your patience while on hold.

The daylight dwindles, twilight spreads, and I,
I cool as I sit quiet in fading light.
Viewed through the wrong end of a telescope
You slowly turn, then disappear from sight.
The silent ending of a tale foretold.
We thank you for your patience while on hold.

Interloper

She knows, she must know I'm here.
Why else work so hard to erase
my fingerprints? Why paint them over?
Why scrape every floor of all trace?

I sit at her table each morning
while she sips her nice cup of tea;
I lounge on her chaise in the evening
in the spot where my bed once held me.

When she unlocks the door I'm behind it
in my old housecoat, poised for escape.
Yet porous and blank as my brain is,
it holds on to this home—so I stay.

Maybe *her* brain is sprung from its sprocket,
ignoring me plain as I stand,
my foot next to hers on the stair step;
on the railing, my hand on her hand.

Rush Hour

Legs scissor in and out
of yellow taxis that swim
the grey streets,
empty-eyed goldfish,
swallowing
and disgorging
their frantic cargo.

Green-haired trio,
bristling with piercings,
ablaze with tattoos,
garish yet docile,
awaits the walk light.

Tall gleaming girl,
all cell phone chatter,
swinging hair,
straight-ahead stride.
Might as well
be a bowling ball.
Men topple
in her wake.

A briefcase is dropped.
Papers loft to the sky,
an offering to the gods of
five o'clock.

ABOUT THE AUTHOR

Kathleen Cochran was born in Munich, Germany. At the age of one year she moved with her parents to Jacksonville, Florida, where she spent her childhood. She received a B.A. in English literature from Mt. Holyoke College, an M.S. in early childhood education from Bank Street College, and an Ed.M. from Teachers College, Columbia University. She was co-creator of the Peaceful Kids Early Childhood Conflict Resolution program at Teachers College. She is the author of *A Community of Learners*, published by Creative Response to Conflict. She has created print, video, and Web-based curriculum materials in language arts, social skills, health, and science. Her poetry has appeared in *Subtropic* and *The Westchester Review.*

Upended is her first published book of poems.

Made in the USA
Middletown, DE
04 November 2020